Knit Dishcloth Sampler

Twelve Nifty
Pattern Stitches

Bobbie Matela, Managing Editor
Carol Wilson Mansfield, Art Director
Mary Ann Frits, Editorial Director
Kathy Wesley, Senior Editor
Sandy Scoville, Pattern Editor
Denise Black and Stephanie Hill, Editorial Staff
Graphic Solutions inc-chgo, Book Design

*For a full-color catalog including books
of crochet and knit designs, write to:*

**American School of Needlework®
Consumer Division**
1455 Linda Vista Drive
San Marcos, CA 92069

or visit us at:
http://www.asnpub.com

Yarn used in this book provided by Lion Brand Yarn Company and Spinrite.

Patterns tested and models made by Eileen McNutt, Susie Adams Steele, and Rita Weiss.

Introduction

Half the fun of knitting is trying something new!

This collection of a dozen dishcloths, each showcasing a different interesting stitch pattern, allows you to try your hand at patterns that may look challenging, but are easier than you might think.

Using just a little worsted weight cotton yarn (rather than enough yarn for a whole sweater), you can experiment with cables and twisted stitches in a small, but useful piece.

Best of all, you'll have a collection of dishcloths that make wonderful hostess gifts or make washing your own dishes less of a chore.

Abbreviations and Symbols

beg . . . . begin(ning)

bl(s) . . . . back loop(s)

C4B . . . . cable four back

C4F . . . . cable four front

CB . . . . cable back

gm(s) . . . . gram(s)

inc . . . . increase(-ing)

K. . . . . knit

lp(s) . . . . loop(s)

oz . . . . ounce(s)

P . . . . purl

patt . . . . pattern

prev . . . . previous

PSSO . . . . . pass slipped stitch over

rem . . . . remain(ing)

rep . . . . repeat(ing)

rnd(s) . . . . round(s)

sk. . . . . skip

sl . . . . slip

sp(s) . . . . space(s)

st(s) . . . . stitch(es)

T4B. . . . . twist four back

T4F . . . . twist four front

T4L . . . . twist four left

T4R. . . . . twist four right

TL . . . . twist left

tog. . . . . together

TR. . . . . twist right

yb . . . . yarn back

yd(s). . . . . yard(s)

yf. . . . . yarn forward

YO . . . . yarn over

* An asterisk is used to mark the beginning of a portion of instructions which will be worked more than once; thus, "rep from ***** twice more" means after working the instructions once, repeat the instructions following the asterisk twice more (3 times in all).

† The dagger identifies a portion of instructions that will be repeated again later in the same row.

— The number after a long dash at the end of a row indicates the number of stitches you should have when the row has been completed.

( ) Parentheses are used to enclose instructions which should be worked the exact number of times specified immediately following the parentheses, such as "**(**K2, P2**)** twice." They are also used to provide additional information to clarify instructions.

A Word About Gauge

Please take the time to work a stitch gauge swatch about 4" x 4". Measure the swatch. If the number of stitches and rows are fewer than indicated under "Gauge" in the pattern, your needles are too large.

Try another swatch with smaller size needles. If the number of stitches and rows are more that indicated under "Gauge" in the pattern, your needles are too small. Try another swatch with larger size needles.

Metric Conversion Charts

INCHES INTO MILLIMETERS & CENTIMETERS (Rounded off slightly)

inches	mm	cm	inches	cm	inches	cm	inches	cm
1/8	3		5	12.5	21	53.5	38	96.5
1/4	6		5 1/2	14	22	56	39	99
3/8	10	1	6	15	23	58.5	40	101.5
1/2	13	1.3	7	18	24	61	41	104
5/8	15	1.5	8	20.5	25	63.5	42	106.5
3/4	20	2	9	23	26	66	43	109
7/8	22	2.2	10	25.5	27	68.5	44	112
1	25	2.5	11	28	28	71	45	114.5
1 1/4	32	3.2	12	30.5	29	73.5	46	117
1 1/2	38	3.8	13	33	30	76	47	119.5
1 3/4	45	4.5	14	35.5	31	79	48	122
2	50	5	15	38	32	81.5	49	124.5
2 1/2	65	6.5	16	40.5	33	84	50	127
3	75	7.5	17	43	34	86.5		
3 1/2	90	9	18	46	35	89		
4	100	10	19	48.5	36	91.5		
4 1/2	115	11.5	20	51	37	94		

mm - millimeter   cm - centimeter

KNITTING NEEDLES CONVERSION CHART

U.S.	0	1		2		3	4	5		6	7	8	9	10	10 1/2			11	13	15
Metric(mm)	2	2 1/4	2 1/2	2 3/4	3	3 1/8	3 1/2	3 3/4	4	4 1/4	4 1/2	5	5 1/4	5 3/4	6 1/2	7	7 1/2	8	9	10

Diamonds

Size:
About 11" x 10½"

Materials:
Worsted weight cotton yarn, 2½ oz (225 yds, 70 gms) white

Note: *Our photographed dishcloth was made with Lily® Sugar'n Cream®, White #1*

Size 8 (5mm) knitting needles, or size required for gauge

Cable needle

Gauge:
In stockinette st (knit one row, purl one row):
9 sts = 2"

Pattern Stitches:

Cable Back (CB):
Sl next 3 sts onto cable needle and hold in back of work, K3, K3 from cable needle—CB made.

Twist Right (TR):
Sl next st onto cable needle and hold in back of work, K3, K1 from cable needle—TR made.

Twist Left (TL):
Sl next 3 sts onto cable needle and hold in front of work, K1, K3 from cable needle—TL made.

Instructions
Cast on 58 sts.

Row 1 (right side):
Knit.

Rows 2 through 5:
Knit.

Row 6:
K4, P50, K4.

Row 7:
* K10, CB (see Pattern Stitches); rep from * twice more; K10.

Row 8 and all even numbered rows through Row 40:
K4, P50, K4.

Row 9:
K9, TR (see Pattern Stitches); TL (see Pattern Stitches); * K8, TR; TL; rep from * once more; K9.

Row 11:
K8, TR; K2, TL; * K6, TR; K2, TL; rep from * once more; K8.

Row 13:
K7, TR; K4, TL; * K4, TR; K4, TL; rep from * once more; K7.

Row 15:
K6, TR; K6, TL; * K2, TR; K6, TL; rep from * once more; K6.

Row 17:
K5; * TR; K8, TL; rep from * twice more; K5.

Row 19:
K18; * CB; K10; rep from * once more; K8.

Rows 21 and 23:
Knit.

Row 25:
Rep Row 19.

Row 27:
K5; * TL; K8, TR; rep from * twice more; K5.

Row 29:
K6, TL; K6, TR; * K2, TL; K6, TR; rep from * once more; K6.

6

Row 31:
K7, TL; K4, TR; * K4, TL; K4, TR; rep from * once more; K7.

Row 33:
K8, TL; K2, TR; * K6, TL; K2, TR; rep from * once more; K8.

Row 35:
K9, TL; TR; * K8, TL; TR; rep from * once more; K9.

Row 37:
Rep Row 7.

Row 39:
Knit.

Row 40:
K4, P50, K4.

Rows 41 through 76:
Rep Rows 5 through 40 once more.

Rows 77 through 79:
Knit.

Bind off.

Honeycomb

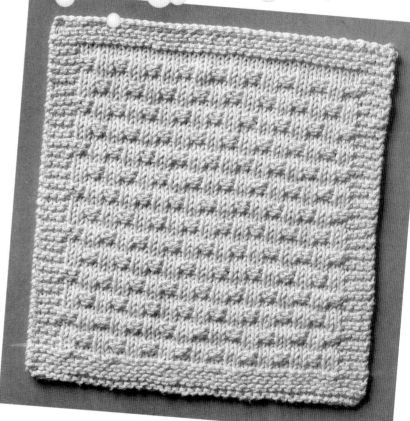

Size:
About 9½" x 10"

Materials:
Worsted weight cotton yarn, 2 oz (180 yds, 56 gms) yellow
Note: Our photographed dishcloth was made with Kitchen Cotton, Sunflower #157.
Size 8 (5mm) knitting needles, or size required for gauge

Gauge:
In stockinette st (knit one row, purl one row):
9 sts = 2"

Instructions
Cast on 42 sts.

Row 1 (right side):
Knit.

Rows 2 through 7:
Knit.

Row 8:
K4, P34, K4.

Row 9:
K6; * P2, K2; rep from * 7 times more; K4.

Row 10:
K4, P2; * K2, P2; rep from * 7 times more; K4.

Row 11:
Knit.

Row 12:
K4, P34, K4.

Row 13:
Rep Row 10.

Row 14:
Rep Row 9.

Row 15:
Knit.

Row 16:
K4, P34, K4.

Rep Rows 9 through 16 until piece measures about 9½" from cast-on row, ending by working a Row 12 or a Row 16.

Next Five Rows:
Knit.

Bind off.

Entwined Cables

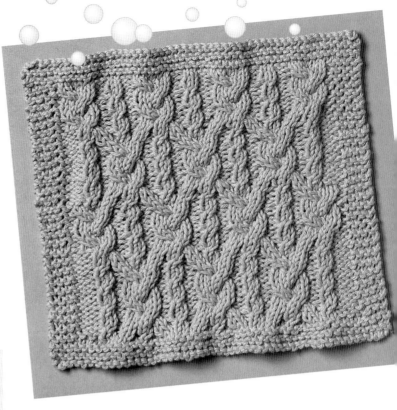

Size:
About 10" x 9¹/₂"

Materials:
Worsted weight cotton yarn, 2¹/₂ oz (225 yds,
 70 gms) green
 Note: *Our photographed dishcloth was made
 with Lily® Sugar 'n Cream®, Light Green #55.*
Size 8 (5mm) knitting needles, or size required
 for gauge
Cable needle

Gauge:
In stockinette st (knit one row, purl one row):
9 sts = 2"

Pattern Stitches:

Cable Back (CB):
Sl next st onto cable needle and hold in back of
work, K1, K1 from cable needle—CB made.

Twist Left (TL):
Sl next 2 sts onto cable needle and hold in front of
work, P1, K2 from cable needle—TL made.

Twist Right (TR):
Sl next st onto cable needle and hold in back of
work, K2, P1 from cable needle—TR made.

Twist Four Left (T4L):
Sl next 2 sts onto cable needle and hold in front of
work, K2, K2 from cable needle—T4L made.

Twist Four Right (T4R):
Sl next 2 sts onto cable needle and hold in back of
work, K2, K2 from cable needle—T4R made.

Instructions
Cast on 52 sts.

Row 1 (right side):
Knit.

Rows 2 through 5:
Knit.

Row 6:
K4, P44, K4.

Row 7:
K4, P3, K2; * TL (see Pattern Stitches); P1, CB (see
Pattern Stitches); P1, TR (see Pattern Stitches); K2;
rep from * twice more; P3, K4.

Row 8:
K7, P2; * K1, P2; rep from * 11 times more; K7.

Row 9:
K4, P3, CB; * P1, TL; K2, TR; P1, CB; rep from * twice
more; P3, K4.

Row 10:
K7, P2; * K2, P6, K2, P2; rep from * twice more; K7.

Row 11:
K4, P3, K2, P2; * T4R (see Pattern Stitches); (K2, P2)
twice; rep from * twice more; P1, K4.

Row 12:
Rep Row 10.

Row 13:
K4, P3, CB; * P2, K2, T4L (see Pattern Stitches); P2, CB;
rep from * twice more; P3, K4.

Row 14:
Rep Row 10.

Row 15:
K4, P3, K2; * P2, K6, P2, K2; rep from * twice more; P3,
K4.

Row 16:
Rep Row 10.

Row 17:
K4, P3, CB; * P2, T4R; K2, P2, CB; rep from * twice more;
P3, K4.

Row 18:
Rep Row 10.

Row 19:
K4, P3, K2; * P2, K2, T4L; P2, K2; rep from * twice more; P3, K4.

Row 20:
Rep Row 10.

Row 21:
K4, P3, CB; * P1, TR; K2, TL; P1, CB; rep from * twice more; P3, K4.

Row 22:
Rep Row 8.

Row 23:
K4, P3, K2; * TR; P1, CB; P1, TL; K2; rep from * twice more; P3, K4.

Row 24:
K5, P6; * K2, P2, K2, P6; rep from * twice more; K5.

Row 25:
K4, P1, T4R; * (K2, P2) twice; T4R; rep from * twice more; K2, P1, K4.

Row 26:
Rep Row 24.

Row 27:
K4, P1, K2, T4L; * P2, CB; P2, K2, T4L; rep from * twice more; P1, K4.

Row 28:
Rep Row 24.

Row 29:
K4, P1, K6; * P2, K2, P2, K6; rep from * twice more; P1, K4.

Row 30:
Rep Row 24.

Row 31:
K4, P1, T4R; K2; * P2, CB; P2, T4R; K2; rep from * twice more; P1, K4.

Row 32:
Rep Row 24.

Row 33:
K4, P1, K2, T4L; * (P2, K2) twice; T4L; rep from * twice more; P1, K4.

Row 34:
Rep Row 24.

Rows 35 through 62:
Rep Rows 7 through 34, once more.

Rows 63 through 67:
Knit.

Bind off.

Chains

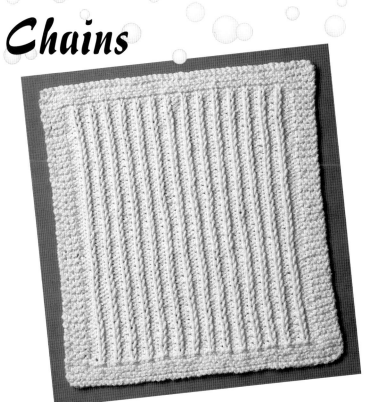

Size:
About 10$\frac{1}{2}$" x 12"

Materials:
Worsted weight cotton yarn, 2$\frac{1}{2}$ oz (225 yds, 70 gms) off white
> ***Note:*** *Our photographed dishcloth was made with Lily® Sugar 'n Cream®, Ivory #7.*

Size 8 knitting needles, or size required for gauge

Gauge:
In stockinette st (knit one row, purl one row):
9 sts = 2"

Instructions
Cast on 52 sts.

Row 1 (right side):
Knit.

Rows 2 through 6:
Knit.

Row 7:
K4, P2; * yb, sl 1 as to purl, yf, P2; rep from * 13 times more; K4.

Row 8:
K6; * P1, K2; rep from * 13 times more; K4.

Rep Rows 7 and 8 until piece measures about 11" from cast-on row.

Next Five Rows:
Knit.

Bind off.

9

Wavy Ribs

Size:
About 10" x 8"

Materials:
Worsted weight cotton yarn, 2¹/₂ oz (225 yds, 70 gms) rust

Note: Our photographed dishcloth was made with Kitchen Cotton, Cinnamon #135.

Size 8 (5mm) knitting needles, or size required for gauge

Cable needle

Gauge:
In stockinette st (knit one row, purl one row): 9 sts = 2"

Pattern Stitches:

Cable Four Back (C4B):
Sl next st onto cable needle and hold in back of work, K3, P1 from cable needle—C4B made.

Cable Four Front (C4F):
Sl next 3 sts onto cable needle and hold in front of work, P1, K3 from cable needle—C4F made.

Instructions
Cast on 50 sts.

Row 1 (right side):
Knit.

Rows 2 through 6:
Knit.

Row 7:
K4, P5, C4B (see Pattern Stitches); * P4, C4B; rep from * 3 times more; P1, K4.

Row 8:
K6; * P3, K5; rep from * 4 times more; K4.

Row 9:
K4; * P4, C4B; rep from * 4 times more; P2, K4.

Row 10:
K7, P3; * K5, P3; rep from * 3 times more; K8.

Row 11:
K4, P3; C4B; * P4, C4B; rep from * 3 times more; P3, K4.

Row 12:
K8, P3; * K5, P3; rep from * 3 times more; K7.

Row 13:
K4, P2; * C4B; P4; rep from * 4 times more; K4.

Row 14:
K4; * K5, P3; rep from * 4 times more; K6.

Row 15:
K4, P1; * C4B; P4; rep from * 4 times more; P1, K4.

Row 16:
K10, P3; * K5, P3; rep from * 3 times more; K5.

Row 17:
K4, P1; * C4F (see Pattern Stitches); P4; rep from * 4 times more; P1, K4.

Row 18:
Rep Row 14.

Row 19:
K4, P2; * C4F; P4; rep from * 4 times more; K4.

Row 20:
Rep Row 12.

Row 21:
K4, P3, C4F; * P4, C4F; rep from * 3 times more; P3, K4.

Row 22:
Rep Row 10.

Row 23:
K4; * P4, C4F; rep from * 4 times more; P2, K4.

Row 24:
Rep Row 8.

Row 25:
K4, P5, C4F; * P4, C4F; rep from * 3 times more; P1, K4.

Row 26:
K5; * P3, K5; rep from * 4 times more; K5.

Rows 27 through 46:
Rep Rows 7 through 26 once more.

Rows 47 through 51:
Knit.

Bind off.

Crisscross

Size:
About 8" x 9"

Materials:
Worsted weight cotton yarn, 2¹/₂ oz (225 yds,
   70 gms) gold
   Note: *Our photographed dishcloth was made*
   with Kitchen Cotton, Maize #186.
Size 8 (5mm) knitting needles, or size required
   for gauge
Cable needle

Gauge:
In stockinette st (knit one row, purl one row):
9 sts = 2"

Pattern Stitches:

Twist Four Right (T4R**):**
Sl next 2 sts onto cable needle and hold in back of
work, K2, K2 from cable needle—T4R made.

Twist Four Back (T4B**):**
Sl next 2 sts onto cable needle and hold in back of
work, K2, P2 from cable needle—T4B made.

Twist Four Front (T4F**):**
Sl next 2 sts onto cable needle and hold in front of
work, P2, K2 from cable needle—T4F made.

Instructions
Cast on 50 sts.

Row 1 (right side**):**
Knit.

Rows 2 through 6:
Knit.

Row 7:
K4, P3, T4R **(see Pattern Stitches)**; ✳ P4, T4R; rep from
✳ 3 times more; P3, K4.

Row 8:
K7, P4; ✳ K4, P4; rep from ✳ 3 times more; K7.

Row 9:
K4, P1; ✳ T4B **(see Pattern Stitches)**; T4F **(see Pattern**
Stitches); rep from ✳ 4 times more; P1, K4.

Row 10:
K5, P2, K4; ✳ P4, K4; rep from ✳ 3 times more; P2, K5.

Row 11:
K4, P1, K2, P4; ✳ T4R; P4; rep from ✳ 3 times more; K2,
P1, K4.

Row 12:
Rep Row 10.

Row 13:
K4, P1; ✳ T4F; T4B; rep from ✳ 4 times more; P1, K4.

Row 14:
Rep Row 8.

Rows 15 through 46:
Rep Rows 7 through 14 four times more.

Rows 47 through 51:
Knit.

Bind off.

Weavings

Size:
About 9½" x 8"

Materials:
Worsted weight cotton yarn, 2½ oz (225 yds,
    70 gms) lavender
    Note: *Our photographed dishcloth was made
    with Kitchen Cotton, Grape #144.*
Size 8 (5mm) knitting needles, or size required
    for gauge
Cable needle

Gauge:
In stockinette st (knit one row, purl one row):
9 sts = 2"

Pattern Stitches:

Twist Four Right (T4R):
Sl next 2 sts onto cable needle and hold in back
of work, K2, K2 from cable needle—T4R made.

Twist Four Left (T4L):
Sl next 2 sts onto cable needle and hold in front of
work, K2, K2 from cable needle—T4L made.

Twist Four Back (T4B):
Sl next 2 sts onto cable needle and hold in back of
work, K2, P2 from cable needle—T4B made.

Twist Four Front (T4F):
Sl next 2 sts onto cable needle and hold in front of
work, P2, K2 from cable needle—T4F made.

Instructions
Cast on 50 sts.

Row 1 (right side):
Knit.

Rows 2 through 6:
Knit.

Row 7:
K4, P3, T4R (see Pattern Stitches); ✱ P4, T4R; rep from
✱ 3 times more; P3, K4.

Row 8:
K7, P4; ✱ K4, P4; rep from ✱ 3 times more; K7.

Row 9:
K4, P1; ✱ T4B (see Pattern Stitches); T4F (see Pattern
Stitches); rep from ✱ 4 times more; P1, K4.

Row 10:
K5, P2, K4; ✱ P4, K4; rep from ✱ 3 times more;
P2, K5.

Row 11:
K4, P1, K2, P4; ✱ T4L (see Pattern Stitches); P4;
rep from ✱ three times more; K2, P1, K4.

Row 12:
Rep Row 10.

Row 13:
K4, P1; ✱ T4F; T4B; rep from ✱ 4 times more; P1, K4.

Row 14:
Rep Row 8.

Rows 15 through 46:
Rep Rows 7 through 14 four times more.

Rows 47 through 51:
Knit.

Bind off.

Cables

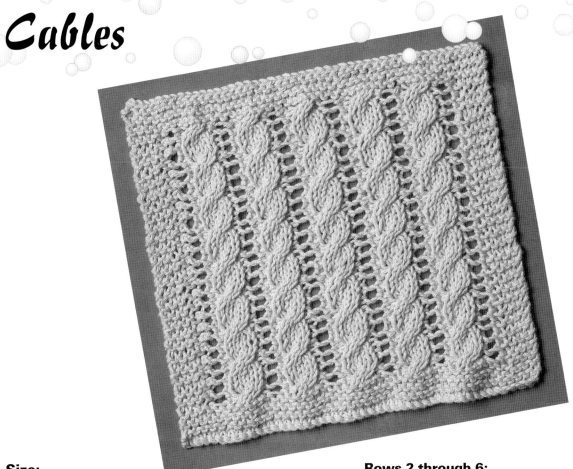

Size:
About 10" x 9"

Materials:
Worsted weight cotton yarn, 2$\frac{1}{2}$ oz (225 yds, 70 gms)
It green

Note: *Our photographed dishcloth was made with Kitchen Cotton, Pistachio #169.*

Size 8 (5mm) knitting needles, or size required for gauge

Cable needle

Gauge:
In stockinette st (knit one row, purl one row):
9 sts = 2"

Pattern Stitch

Twist Four Right (T4R):
SI next 2 sts onto cable needle and hold in back of work, K2, K2 from cable needle—T4R made.

Instructions
Cast on 46 sts.

Row 1 (right side):
Knit.

Rows 2 through 6:
Knit.

Row 7:
K4, P3; * K4, P3; rep from * 4 times more; K4.

Row 8:
K5, yf, K2 tog; * P4, K1, yf, K2 tog; rep from * 4 times more; K4.

Row 9:
K4, P3; * T4R (see Pattern Stitch); P3; rep from * 4 times more; K4.

Row 10:
Rep Row 8.

Rows 11 and 12:
Rep Rows 7 and 8.

Rep Rows 7 through 12 until piece measures about 9$\frac{1}{2}$" from cast-on row, ending by working a Row 10.

Next Five Rows:
Knit.

Bind off.

Stripes

Size:
About 11" x 9"

Materials:
Worsted weight cotton yarn, 2 oz (180 yds, 56 gms)
   lt green
   Note: *Our photographed dishcloth was made with Kitchen Cotton, Lime #174*
Size 8 knitting needles, or size required for gauge

Gauge:
In stockinette st (knit one row, purl one row):
9 sts = 2"

Instructions
Cast on 50 sts.

Row 1 (right side**):**
Knit.

Rows 2 through 6:
Knit.

Row 7:
K4, P2; * K3, P2; rep from * 8 times more; K4.

Row 8:
K6; * P1, K1, P1, K2; rep from * 8 times more; K4.

Rep Rows 7 and 8 until piece measures about 9$\frac{1}{2}$" from cast-on row.

Next Five Rows:
Knit.

Bind off.

Columns

Size:
About 10¹/₂" x 9"

Materials:
Worsted weight cotton yarn, 2¹/₂ oz (225 yds, 70 gms) fuchsia

Note: Our photographed dishcloth was made with Kitchen Cotton, Boysenberry #142.

Size 8 (5mm) knitting needles, or size required for gauge

Gauge:
In stockinette st (knit one row, purl one row):
9 sts = 2"

Instructions
Cast on 47 sts.

Row 1 (right side):
Knit.

Rows 2 through 6:
Knit.

Row 7:
K4, P3; * sl 1 as to purl, yb, K1, yf, sl 1 as to purl, P3; rep from * 5 times more; K4.

Row 8:
K7; * P3, K3; rep from * 5 times more; K4.

Row 9:
K4; * P3, K1, yf, sl 1 as to purl, yb, K1; rep from * 5 times more; P3, K4.

Row 10:
Rep Row 8.

Rep Rows 7 through 10 until piece measures about 9¹/₂" from cast-on row, ending by working a Row 10.

Next Five Rows:
Knit.

Bind off.

Basketweave

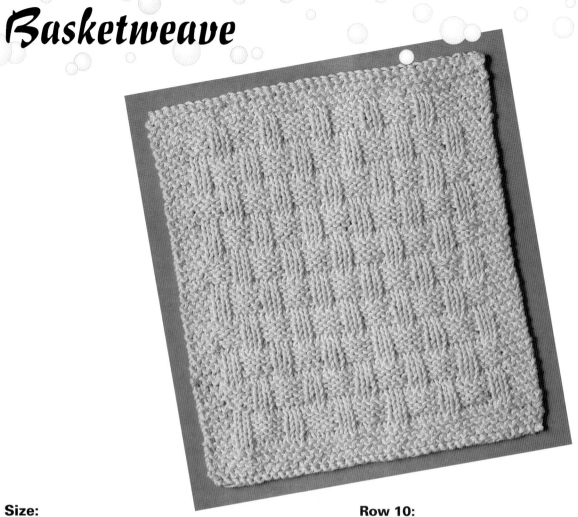

Size:
About 9" x 10½"

Materials:
Worsted weight cotton yarn, 2½ oz (225 yds, 70 gms) pink
> ***Note:*** *Our photographed dishcloth was made with Kitchen Cotton, Pastel Pink #101*

Size 8 knitting needles, or size required for gauge

Gauge:
In stockinette st (knit one row, purl one row): 9 sts = 2"

Instructions
Cast on 40 sts.

Row 1 (right side**):**
Knit.

Rows 2 through 7:
Knit.

Row 8:
K4, P32, K4.

Row 9:
K6; ***** P4, K2; rep from ***** 4 times more; K4.

Row 10:
* K4, P2; rep from ***** 5 times more; K4.

Rows 11 and 12:
Rep Rows 9 and 10 once more.

Row 13:
Knit.

Row 14:
K4, P32, K4.

Row 15:
K4, P3; ***** K2, P4; rep from ***** 3 times more; K2, P3, K4.

Row 16:
K7; ***** P2, K4; rep from ***** 3 times more; P2, K7.

Rows 17 and 18:
Rep Rows 15 and 16 once more.

Rows 19 through 66:
Rep Rows 7 through 18 four times more.

Rows 67 through 72.
Knit.

Bind off.